FROM THE FILMS OF

Harry Potter™

Hidden Hogwarts™

Scratch Magic

SCHOLASTIC INC.

This book is a work of fiction. Names, characters, places, and incidents
are either the product of the author's imagination or are used fictitiously,
and any resemblance to actual persons, living or dead, business
establishments, events, or locales is entirely coincidental.

ISBN 978-1-338-24610-0

10 9 8 7 6   20 21 22 23 24

Printed in China
First printing 2018

Design and additional illustrations by Carolyn Bull

Revelio!

In the wizarding world, things are not always as they seem. Witches and wizards can brew a potion to transform into someone else. The Hogwarts carriages that appear to move by themselves are actually pulled by mysterious creatures. What looks like a plain brick wall is the entrance to a street full of magical shops.

Now it's your turn to reveal some magic! Turn the page and follow the prompts to draw, doodle, and unveil colorful patterns and memorable scenes inspired by the Harry Potter films.

At Hogwarts, which house is known for bravery, nerve, chivalry, courage, and daring? Scratch to reveal the house and four of its most notable students.

Just because you can't see something doesn't mean it's not there. Luna Lovegood is one of the few people at Hogwarts who can see Thestrals, rare and gentle creatures. Scratch and see who and what is hidden on the next page.

When Cornish pixies get loose in the Defense Against the Dark Arts classroom, Hermione uses the Immobulus spell. Scratch to freeze the little troublemakers in midair!

In the game of Quidditch, a Seeker's job is to catch the Golden Snitch. First, scratch to reveal Seekers Harry and Draco flying across the Quidditch pitch.

Then scratch to find the Snitch. Look out, it moves fast!

Scratch to reveal the sparkle of Luna's Spectrespecs. Then draw what you think Wrackspurts look like as seen through her glasses.

In the wizarding world, magical transformation happens all the time. Tonks, a Metamorphmagus, can transform any part of her appearance at will—like giving herself a duck beak! Both Sirius Black and Professor McGonagall are Animagi. Scratch to reveal what animals they transform into. Then see which Dark witch Hermione transforms into when she drinks Polyjuice Potion.

In the wizarding world, many witches and wizards choose to bring a pet to school with them, most of which are owls, rats, cats, or toads. Harry has a snowy owl named Hedwig. Scratch away his friends' outlines to reveal each of their pets!

Harry's Patronus is a stag. Scratch the white away to summon a shimmering Patronus for Ron, Hermione, and Luna.

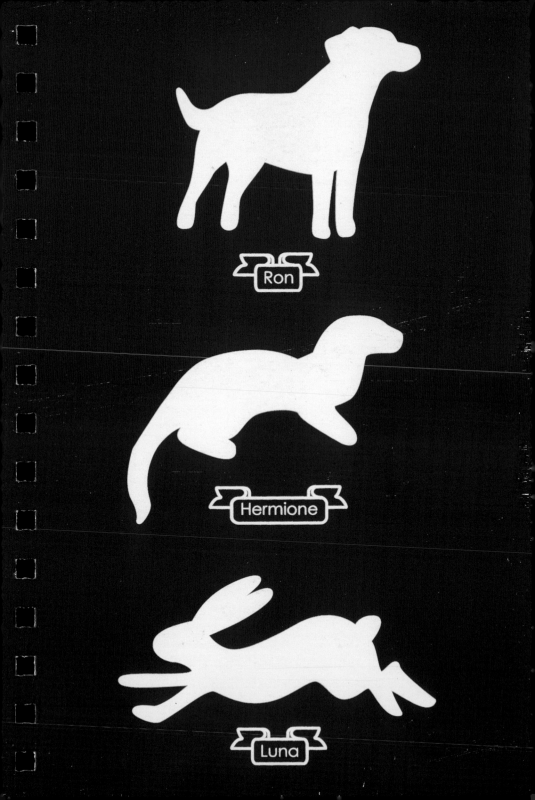

Dobby the house-elf must follow orders from the cruel Malfoy family. He can only be freed if his master presents him with clothing. Scratch to find a sock for Dobby so he can be a free elf once and for all!

Harry is on the run after Voldemort secretly takes control of the Ministry of Magic and labels him as "Undesirable No. 1."

Harry's not the only innocent person who has had to hide from the Ministry. Scratch to reveal another wanted wizard.

Harry, Ron, and Hermione use Harry's Invisibility Cloak to sneak around Hogwarts after hours—but sometimes it's hard to make sure they're fully concealed. Scratch to reveal which member of the trio is hiding—and where!

Ron is nervous to compete in his first Quidditch match. Draw a sign to cheer him on from the Gryffindor section in the stands!

Then draw more signs for students playing on other house teams.

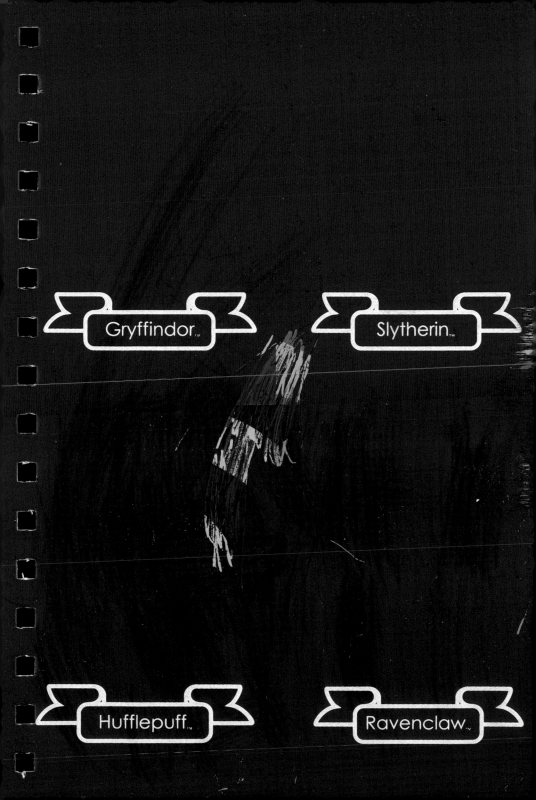

Gryffindor™

Slytherin™

Hufflepuff™

Ravenclaw™

In Divination class, Professor Trelawney teaches her students how to predict the future. Draw what you think your future holds inside the crystal ball.

The Order of the Phoenix is a secret group of witches and wizards who fight Voldemort and his Death Eaters. Albus Dumbledore is one of its most powerful members—scratch to reveal the identity of other important members.

The Marauder's Map, discovered in Filch's office by Fred and George Weasley, is a magical parchment that knows the locations of everyone in Hogwarts. Say "I solemnly swear that I am up to no good," and scratch to reveal Hogwarts' other notable mischief makers!

Scratch to locate the flying key that leads Harry to the Sorcerer's Stone. Hurry! He must find the key before Voldemort does.

Professor Snape is always brewing up some new potions. Scratch inside the potion bottles to reveal what potion is inside each one.

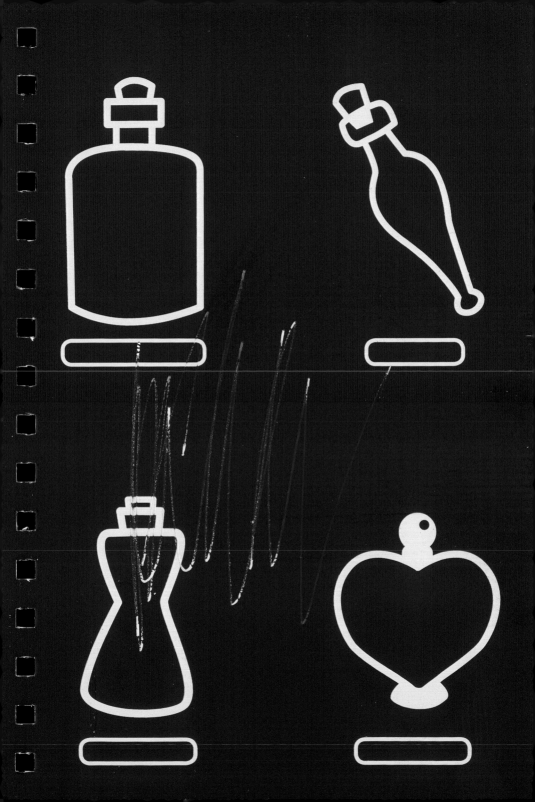

Hagrid loves magical creatures, even the ones most witches and wizards would consider a little bit dangerous. Reveal all the different pets Hagrid has kept on the next page.

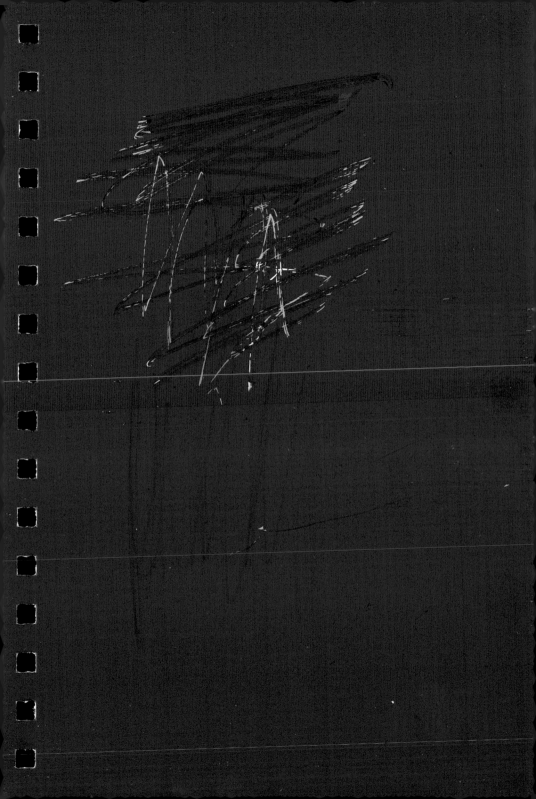

Lumos is the spell used to produce light from a wand. Scratch the letters to bring some light to this page!

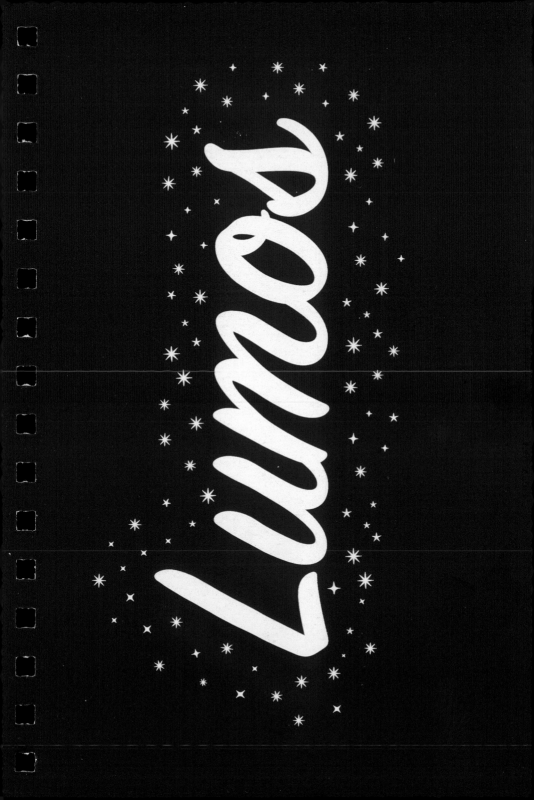

Scratch the Hogwarts crest to
reveal the animal that represents
each of the four houses.